SHAKESPEARE, W.

Julius Caesar ; abridged by Leon
Garfield

STRATFORD AREA LIBRARY,
12, HENLEY STREET,
STRATFORD-ON-AVON,
WARWICKSHIRE,
CV37 6PZ
Tel. 292209

WELLESBOURNE.
395

11 MAY 2009

21. JUL

29 OCT 2008

18. MAY 02

07. SEP 05.

This item is to be returned on or before the latest date
above.

It may be borrowed for a further period if not in demand.

Shakespeare The Animated Tales is a multinational venture conceived by S4C, Channel 4 Wales. Produced in Russia, Wales and England, the series has been financed by S4C and the BBC (UK), Christmas Films (Russia), Home Box Office (USA) and Fujisankei (Japan).

Academic Panel
Professor Stanley Wells
Dr Rex Gibson

Educational Adviser
Michael Marland

Publishing Editor and Co-ordinator
Jane Fior

Book Design
Fiona Macmillan and Ness Wood

Animation Director for *Julius Caesar*
Yuri Kulakov of Christmas Films, Moscow

Series Editors
Martin Lamb and Penelope Middelboe, Right Angle, Tenby, Wales

Executive Producers
Christopher Grace (S4C)
Elizabeth Babakhina (Christmas Films)

Associate Producer
Theresa Plummer Andrews (BBC)

First published in 1994
by William Heinemann Ltd
an imprint of Reed Consumer Books Ltd
Michelin House, 81 Fulham Road, London SW3 6RB
and Auckland, Melbourne, Singapore and Toronto
Copyright © Shakespeare Animated Films/Christmas Films 1994

ISBN 0 434 96780 7

A CIP catalogue record for this title is available
from the British Library

Printed and bound in the UK by BPC Paulton Books Limited

The publishers would like to thank Paul Cox
for the series logo illustration,
Carol Kemp for her calligraphy,
Theo Crosby for the use of his painting of the Globe,
and Rosa Fior and Celia Salisbury Jones
for their help on the books.

Shakespeare
THE ANIMATED TALES

JULIUS CAESAR

ABRIDGED BY LEON GARFIELD

ILLUSTRATED BY VICTOR CHUGUYEVSKI

YURI KULAKOV, AND GALINA MELKO

HEINEMANN YOUNG BOOKS

William Shakespeare

Martin Droeshout sculpsit London.

WILLIAM SHAKESPEARE

NEXT TO GOD, A wise man once said, Shakespeare created most. In the thirty-seven plays that are his chief legacy to the world – and surely no-one ever left a richer! – human nature is displayed in all its astonishing variety.

He has enriched the stage with matchless comedies, tragedies, histories, and, towards the end of his life, with plays that defy all description, strange plays that haunt the imagination like visions.

His range is enormous: kings and queens, priests, princes and merchants, soldiers, clowns and drunkards, murderers, pimps, whores, fairies, monsters and pale, avenging ghosts 'strut and fret their hour upon the stage'. Murders and suicides abound; swords flash, blood flows, poison drips, and lovers sigh; yet there is always time for old men to talk of growing apples and for gardeners to discuss the weather.

In the four hundred years since they were written, they have become known and loved in every land; they are no longer the property of one country and one people, they are the priceless possession of the world.

His life, from what we know of it, was not astonishing. The stories that have attached themselves to him are remarkable only for their ordinariness: poaching deer, sleeping off a drinking bout under a wayside tree. There are no duels, no loud, passionate loves, no excesses of any kind. He was not one of your unruly geniuses whose habits are more interesting than their works. From all accounts, he was of a gentle, honourable disposition, a good businessman, and a careful father.

He was born on April 23rd 1564, to John and Mary Shakespeare of Henley Street, Stratford-upon-Avon. He was their third child and first son. When he was four or five he began his education at the local petty school. He left the local grammar school when he was about fourteen, in all probability to help in his father's glove-making shop. When he was eighteen, he married Anne Hathaway, who lived in a nearby village. By the time he was twenty-one, he was the father of three children, two daughters and a son.

Then, it seems, a restless mood came upon him. Maybe he travelled, maybe he was, as some say, a schoolmaster in the country; but at some time during the next seven years, he went to London and found employment in the theatre. When he was twenty-eight, he was already well enough known as an actor and playwright to excite the spiteful envy of a rival, who referred to him as 'an upstart crow'.

He mostly lived and worked in London until his mid-forties, when he returned to his family and home in Stratford, where he remained in prosperous circumstances until his death on April 23rd 1616, his fifty-second birthday.

He left behind him a widow, two daughters (his son died in childhood), and the richest imaginary world ever created by the human mind.

LEON GARFIELD

The list of the plays contained in the First Folio of 1623. This was the first collected edition of Shakespeare's plays and was gathered together by two of his fellow actors, John Hemmings and Henry Condell.

A CATALOGVE

of the feuerall Comedies, Histories, and Tragedies contained in this Volume.

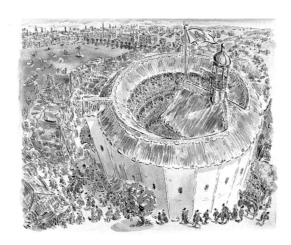

The Theatre in Shakespeare's Day

IN 1989 AN ARCHAEOLOGICAL discovery was made on the south bank of the Thames that sent shivers of delight through the theatre world. A fragment of Shakespeare's own theatre, the Globe, where many of his plays were first performed, had been found.

This discovery has fuelled further interest in how Shakespeare himself conceived and staged his plays. We know a good deal already, and archaeology as well as documentary research will no doubt reveal more, but although we can only speculate on some of the details, we have a good idea of what the Elizabethan theatre-goer saw, heard and smelt when he went to see a play by William Shakespeare at the Globe.

It was an entirely different experience from anything we know today. Modern theatres have roofs to keep out the weather. If it rained on the Globe, forty per cent of the play-goers got wet. Audiences today sit on cushioned seats, and usually (especially if the play is by Shakespeare) watch and listen in respectful silence. In the Globe, the floor of the theatre was packed with a riotous crowd of garlic-reeking apprentices, house servants and artisans, who had each paid a penny to stand for the entire duration of the play, to buy nuts and apples from the food-sellers, to refresh themselves with bottled ale, relieve themselves, perhaps, into buckets by the back wall, to talk, cheer, catcall, clap and hiss if the play did not please them.

In the galleries that rose in curved tiers around the inside of the building sat those who could afford to pay two pennies for a seat, and the benefits of a roof over their heads. Here, the middle ranking citizens, the merchants, the sea captains, the clerks from the Inns of Court, would sit crammed into their small eighteen inch space and look down upon the 'groundlings' below. In the 'Lords' room', the rich and the great, noblemen and women, courtiers and foreign ambassadors had to pay sixpence each for the relative comfort and luxury of their exclusive position directly above the stage, where they smoked tobacco, and overlooked the rest.

We are used to a stage behind an arch, with wings on either side, from which the actors come on and into which they disappear. In the Globe, the stage was a platform thrusting out into the middle of the floor, and the audience, standing in the central yard, surrounded it on three sides. There were no wings. Three doors at the back of the stage were used for all exits and entrances. These were sometimes covered by a curtain, which could be used as a prop.

Today we sit in a darkened theatre or cinema, and look at a brilliantly lit stage or screen, or we sit at home in a small, private world of our own, watching a luminous television screen. The close-packed, rowdy crowd at the Globe, where the play started at two o'clock in the afternoon, had no artificial light to enhance their illusion. It was the words that moved them. They came to listen, rather than to see.

No dimming lights announced the start of the play. A blast from a trumpet and three sharp knocks warned the audience that the action was about to begin. In the broad daylight, the actor could see the audience as clearly as the audience could see him. He spoke directly to the crowd, and held them with his eyes, following their reactions. He could play up to the raucous laughter that greeted the comical, bawdy scenes, and gauge the emotional response to the higher flights of poetry. Sometimes he even improvised speeches of his own. He was surrounded by, enfolded by, his audience.

The stage itself would seem uncompromisingly bare to our eyes. There was no scenery. No painted backdrops suggested a forest, or a castle, or the sumptuous interior of a palace. Shakespeare painted the scenery with his words, and the imagination of the audience did the rest.

Props were brought onto the stage only when they were essential for the action. A bed would be carried on when a character needed to lie on it. A throne would be let down from above when a king needed to sit on it. Torches and lanterns would suggest that it was dark, but the main burden of persuading an audience, at three o'clock in the afternoon, that it was in fact the middle of the night, fell upon the language.

In our day, costume designers create a concept as part of the production of a play into which each costume fits. Shakespeare's actors were responsible for their own costumes. They would use what was to hand in the 'tiring house' (dressing room), or supplement it out of their own pockets. Classical, medieval and Tudor clothes could easily appear side by side in the same play.

No women actors appeared on a public stage until many years after

The Workes of William Shakespeare,

containing all his Comedies, Histories, and
Tragedies : Truely set forth, according to their first
ORIGINALL.

The Names of the Principall Actors
in all these Playes.

William Shakespeare.	Samuel Gilburne.
Richard Burbadge.	Robert Armin.
John Hemmings.	William Ostler.
Augustine Phillips.	Nathan Field.
William Kempt.	John Underwood.
Thomas Poope.	Nicholas Tooley.
George Bryan.	William Ecclestone.
Henry Condell.	Joseph Taylor.
William Slye.	Robert Benfield.
Richard Cowly.	Robert Goughe.
John Lowine.	Richard Robinson.
Samuell Crosse.	Iohn Shancke.
Alexander Cooke.	Iohn Rice.

Shakespeare's death, for at that time it would have been considered shameless. The parts of young girls were played by boys. The parts of older women were played by older men.

In 1613 the Globe theatre was set on fire by a spark from a cannon during a performance of Henry VIII, and it burnt to the ground. The actors, including Shakespeare himself, dug into their own pockets and paid for it to be rebuilt. The new theatre lasted until 1642, when it closed again. Now, in the 1990s, the Globe is set to rise again as a committed band of actors, scholars and enthusiasts are raising the money to rebuild Shakespeare's theatre in its original form a few yards from its previous site.

From the time when the first Globe theatre was built until today, Shakespeare's plays have been performed in a vast variety of languages, styles, costumes and techniques, on stage, on film, on television and in animated film. Shakespeare himself, working within the round wooden walls of his theatre, would have been astonished by it all.

PATRICK SPOTTISWOODE
Director of Education,
Globe Theatre Museum

From this list of actors, we can see that William Shakespeare not only wrote plays but also acted in them. The Globe theatre, where these actors performed, is now being rebuilt close to its original site on the south bank of the river Thames.

SHAKESPEARE TODAY

SHAKESPEARE IS ALIVE TODAY! Although William Shakespeare the man lies long buried in Stratford-upon-Avon parish church, he lives on in countless millions of hearts and minds.

Imagine that cold April day in 1616. The small funeral procession labours slowly along Church Street. Huge black horses draw the wooden cart bearing the simple coffin. On the coffin, a few daffodils and primroses, plucked only minutes before from the garden of New Place, gravely nod with each jolt and jar of the rutted road.

Most of Stratford's citizens have turned out, muffled against the biting wind, to see the last appearance of their wealthy neighbour. You couldn't call it a crowd. Just small respectful groups clustering the dry places on the roadside, careful to avoid the mud splashed up by the great hooves of the lumbering horses.

Men and women briefly bow their heads as the dead man and the black-clad mourners pass. The townspeople share their opinions, as neighbours do. "He used to do some acting, didn't he?" "Made a lot of money in London. Writing plays, I think." "Used to come home once a year to see his family, but nobody here really knew a lot about Master Shakespeare." "Wasn't he a poet?" "Big landowner hereabouts anyway. All those fields over at Welcombe."

Past the Guild Chapel where he had worshipped as a boy. Past the school where long ago his imagination was fired by language. At the churchyard gate, under the sad elms, six men effortlessly heave the coffin on to their shoulders. William Shakespeare is about to enter his parish church for the last time.

Nobody at that long ago funeral guessed that they were saying goodbye to a man who would become the most famous Englishman of his age – perhaps of all time.

Shakespeare lives on. He weaves familiar themes into his tales: the conflicts between parents and children, love at first sight, the power struggles of war and politics. His language is heard everywhere. If you ever call someone 'a blinking idiot' or 'a tower of strength', or describe them as 'tongue-tied', or suffering from 'green-eyed jealousy', or being 'dead as a doornail', you are speaking the language of Shakespeare.

If you say 'it was Greek to me' or 'parting is such sweet sorrow', or that something is 'too much of a good thing' and that you 'have not slept one wink', the words of Shakespeare are alive in your mouth. Shakespeare's language has a power all of its own, rich in emotional intensity. Because he was a poet who wrote plays, he could make even the simplest words utterly memorable. All around the world people know Hamlet's line 'To be or not to be, that is the question.'

Shakespeare is still performed today because of the electrifying power of his storytelling. Whether his story is about love or murder, or kings and queens, he keeps you on the edge of your seat wanting to know what happens next.

He created well over nine hundred characters in his plays. However large or small the part, each character springs vividly to life in performance. They live in our imagination because they are so much like people today. They experience the same emotions that everyone feels and recognises: love, jealousy, fear, courage, ambition, pride ... and a hundred others.

In every play, Shakespeare invites us to imagine what the characters are like, and for nearly four hundred years people have accepted Shakespeare's invitation. The plays have been re-imagined in very many ways. They have been shortened, added to, and set in very different periods of history. They have been translated into many languages and performed all over the world. Shakespeare lives because all persons in every age and every society can make their own interpretations and performances of Shakespeare.

The creators of *The Animated Tales* have re-imagined *Julius Caesar* in a 26 minute animated film. You too can make your own living Shakespeare. Read the text that follows, and watch the video. Then try reading the play either by yourself, changing your voice to suit the different characters, or with friends, and record it on a tape recorder. If you have a toy theatre, try staging it with characters and scenery that you make and paint yourself. Or collect together a cast and create your own production for your family and friends.

Dr Rex Gibson

Dr Rex Gibson is the director of the Shakespeare and Schools Project which is part of the Institute of Education at the University of Cambridge.
   In 1994 he was awarded the Sam Wanamaker International Shakespeare Award for his outstanding contribution to the world's knowledge of the works of Shakespeare.

What They Said of Him

One will ever find, in searching his works, new cause for astonishment and admiration.

Goethe

Shakespeare was a writer of all others the most calculated to make his readers better as well as wiser.

Samuel Taylor Coleridge

An overstrained enthusiasm is more pardonable with respect to Shakespeare than the want of it; for our admiration cannot easily surpass his genius.

William Hazlitt

It required three hundred years for England to begin to hear those two words that the whole world cries in her ear – William Shakespeare.

Victor Hugo

He has left nothing to be said about nothing or anything.

John Keats

The stream of time, which is continually washing the dissoluble fabrics of other poets, passes without injury by the adamant of Shakespeare.

Samuel Johnson

JULIUS CAESAR

The Tragedy of Julius Caesar has been called the greatest play about politics ever written. It is a tale of envy, pride and bloated ambition, of treachery and murder. It is the story of four great men and their struggle for power: of Brutus, a good man, who, for what he believes to be the best of reasons, commits the worst of crimes; of Cassius, 'lean and hungry' Cassius, whose love for his friend Brutus causes him to override his own better judgement and so lead his cause to ruin; of Mark Antony, the 'masker and reveller', who is yet the cleverest and most ruthless politician of them all; and it is the story of Julius Caesar himself, a man who has come to believe so much in his own greatness that he thinks himself a god – "Wilt thou lift up Olympus?" he demands of those who kneel before him to beg for mercy for a friend; and the next instant he perishes under a raging hail of knives …

THE CHARACTERS IN THE PLAY
in order of appearance

A SOOTHSAYER	
JULIUS CAESAR	
CASSIUS	*a conspirator against Julius Caesar*
BRUTUS	*a conspirator against Julius Caesar*
MARK ANTONY	*a general*
CASCA	*a conspirator against Julius Caesar*
CINNA	*a conspirator against Julius Caesar*
LUCIUS	*servant to Brutus*
DEDIUS	*a conspirator against Julius Caesar*
METELLUS	*a conspirator against Julius Caesar*
TREBONIUS	*a conspirator against Julius Caesar*
PORTIA	*wife to Brutus*
CALPHURNIA	*wife to Caesar*
A SENATOR	
FOUR PLEBEIANS	
CINNA	*the poet*
OCTAVIUS	*a general*
THE GHOST OF CAESAR	
PINDARUS	*servant to Cassius*
STRATO	*servant to Brutus*
	Servants, townspeople and soldiers

The curtain rises on a great procession through the streets of Rome. The whole city waits to cheer Julius Caesar, ruler of the world, as he returns in triumph from another glorious victory. Calphurnia, his wife, and all the great ones of Rome follow after him like faithful dogs. Suddenly, a voice cries out.

SOOTHSAYER	Caesar!
CAESAR	Speak. Caesar is turned to hear.
SOOTHSAYER	Beware the ides of March.

The soothsayer is brought before Caesar.

CAESAR	What say'st thou to me now? Speak once again.
SOOTHSAYER	Beware the ides of March.
CAESAR	(*staring at the soothsayer*) He is a dreamer. Let us leave him. Pass.

The procession passes on. Brutus and Cassius remain behind. They lean against the plinth of a huge statue of Caesar, which dwarfs them. There are images of Caesar all around.

CASSIUS	Brutus, I have not from your eyes that gentleness and show of love as I was wont to have.
BRUTUS	Poor Brutus, with himself at war, forgets the shows of love to other men. (*There is a sound of distant shouting.*) What means this shouting? I do fear the people choose Caesar for their king.

CASSIUS   Ay, do you fear it? Then must I think you would not have it so.

BRUTUS   I would not, Cassius; yet I love him well.

There is another shout.

CASSIUS   Why, man, he doth bestride the narrow world like a Colossus, and we petty men walk under his huge legs, and peep about to find ourselves dishonourable graves. What should be in that 'Caesar'? Why should that name be sounded more than yours?

BRUTUS   Caesar is returning!

Caesar enters, followed by his retinue, which includes his friend Mark Antony. He looks angry, and his followers disturbed.

CAESAR   Antonius!

ANTONY   Caesar?

CAESAR Let me have men about me that are fat, sleek-headed men and such as sleep a-nights. Yond Cassius has a lean and hungry look, he thinks too much; such men are dangerous.

ANTONY Fear him not, Caesar, he's not dangerous. He is a noble Roman and well given.

CAESAR Would he were fatter! but I fear him not.

Caesar raises his arm. Trumpets sound, and the procession continues. Casca stays.

BRUTUS Casca, tell us what hath chanced today, that Caesar looks so sad.

CASCA Why, there was a crown offered him. He put it by; but to my thinking, he would fain have had it.

CASSIUS Who offered him the crown?

CASCA Mark Antony.

BRUTUS	What was the second noise for?
CASCA	Why for that too; then he put it by again, but to my thinking he was very loath to lay his fingers off it. As he refused it, the rabblement hooted, and uttered such a deal of stinking breath, that it had, almost, choked Caesar, for he fell down at it.
BRUTUS	'Tis very like; he hath the falling sickness.
CASSIUS	No, Caesar hath it not; but you, and I, and honest Casca, we have the falling sickness.
CASCA	I know not what you mean by that. Farewell, both.

He goes.

BRUTUS	Tomorrow, if you please to speak with me, come home to me, and I will wait for you.
CASSIUS	I will do so; till then, think of the world.

Brutus leaves. Cassius is left alone.

CASSIUS	Well, Brutus, thou art noble; yet I see thy honourable mettle may be wrought; for who so firm that cannot be seduced?

A wild night torn by thunder and lightning. Cassius enters, hastening along a streaming, glaring street. A shadowy figure meets him. It is Casca.

CASSIUS	Who's there?
CASCA	A Roman.
CASSIUS	Casca, by your voice.
CASCA	Cassius, what night is this! Whoever knew the heavens menace so?
CASSIUS	Those that have known the earth so full of faults.
CASCA	They say the senators tomorrow mean to establish Caesar as a king.

CASSIUS   I know where I will wear this dagger then: Cassius from
           bondage will deliver Cassius.

CASCA   So will I. Hold, my hand.

*They clasp hands. The thunder and lightning grow more
violent. Cinna enters.*

CASCA   Stand close a while.

CASSIUS   'Tis Cinna. He is a friend. (*The conspirators huddle close together.*)

CINNA   O Cassius, if you could but win the noble Brutus to our party –

CASSIUS   Good Cinna, take this paper, and throw this in at his window. Three parts of him is ours already, and the man entire upon the next encounter yields him ours!

Cinna goes.

Brutus is walking in his orchard. The fury of the heavens has increased and the dark fabric of the sky is ripped apart by comets and shooting stars.

BRUTUS   It must be by his death. And for my part I know no personal cause to spurn at him for the general. He would be crowned; how that might change his nature. Crown him? – that – and then I grant we put a sting in him. Therefore think of him as a serpent's egg and kill him in the shell.

His servant Lucius enters.

LUCIUS   The taper burneth in your closet, sir. Searching the window for a flint, I found this paper. (*He gives him a scroll.*)

BRUTUS   Is not tomorrow, boy, the ides of March?

LUCIUS   (*nodding in the affirmative*) Sir, March is wasted fifteen days.

There is knocking on the gate.

BRUTUS   Go to the gate, somebody knocks.

Lucius leaves. Brutus opens the scroll and reads.

'Brutus, thou sleep'st. Awake and see thyself! Speak, strike, redress!' Between the acting of a dreadful thing and the first motion, all the interim is like a phantasma or a hideous dream.

Cassius enters, with Decius, Casca, Cinna, Metellus and Trebonius. These last are all cloaked and hooded.

CASSIUS   Good morrow, Brutus.

BRUTUS   Know I these men that come along with you?

CASSIUS   Yes, every man of them.

Cassius reveals himself.

BRUTUS   Give me your hands all over, one by one.

DECIUS   Shall no man else be touched but only Caesar?

CASSIUS   Decius, well urged. I think it is not meet Mark Antony, so well beloved of Caesar, should outlive Caesar.

BRUTUS   Our course will seem too bloody, to cut the head off and then hack the limbs. Let's be sacrificers, but not butchers, Cassius. And for Mark Antony, think not of him.

CASSIUS   Yet I fear him.

TREBONIUS   Let him not die.

CASSIUS   But it is doubtful yet whether Caesar will come forth today or no, for he is superstitious grown of late.

DECIUS   Never fear that. I can o'ersway him, and I will bring him to the Capitol.

A clock strikes three.

TREBONIUS   'Tis time to part.

The conspirators leave. Brutus is left alone. Presently his wife, Portia, comes out of the house and approaches him.

PORTIA   Brutus, my lord!

BRUTUS   Wherefore rise you now?

PORTIA   Dear my lord, make me acquainted with your cause of grief.

BRUTUS   Portia, I am not well in health, and that is all.

PORTIA   No, my Brutus, you have some sick offence within your mind and, upon my knees I charm you, by all your vows of love, that you unfold to me, why you are heavy, and what men tonight have had resort to you, who hid their faces even from the darkness. (*She kneels.*)

BRUTUS   Kneel not, gentle Portia.

PORTIA   I should not need, if you were gentle Brutus. Dwell I but in the suburbs of your good pleasure? If it be no more, Portia is Brutus' harlot, not his wife.

BRUTUS   You are my true and honourable wife, and by and by thy bosom shall partake the secrets of my heart.

It is morning and another wife is filled with fears for her husband. In Caesar's house, Calphurnia pleads with him to stay at home.

CALPHURNIA   What mean you, Caesar? You shall not stir out of your house today.

CAESAR   Caesar shall forth.

CALPHURNIA	I never stood on ceremonies, yet now they fright me. There is one within recounts most horrid sights. A lioness hath whelped in the streets, and graves have yawned and yielded up their dead; fierce fiery warriors fight upon the clouds, which drizzled blood upon the Capitol.
CAESAR	These predictions are to the world in general as to Caesar.
CALPHURNIA	When beggars die, there are no comets seen; the heavens themselves blaze forth the death of princes.
CAESAR	Cowards die many times before their deaths; the valiant never taste of death but once.
CALPHURNIA	Alas, my lord, your wisdom is consumed in confidence. Call it my fear that keeps you in the house and not your own.

She kneels. Caesar smiles indulgently.

CAESAR	For thy humour, I will stay at home.

Decius enters.

DECIUS	Caesar, all hail!
CAESAR	Decius, you are come in very happy time to bear my greetings to the senators, and tell them that I will not come today.
DECIUS	Most mighty Caesar, let me know some cause.

CAESAR   The cause is in my will, I will not come: that is enough to satisfy the senate. But because I love you I will let you know. Calphurnia here, my wife, stays me at home. She dreamt tonight she saw my statue, which, like a fountain with an hundred spouts, did run pure blood, and many lusty Romans came smiling and did bathe their hands in it.

DECIUS   This dream is all amiss interpreted, it signifies that from you great Rome shall suck reviving blood.

CAESAR   And this way have you well expounded it.

DECIUS   And know it now: the senate have concluded to give this day a crown to mighty Caesar. If you shall send them word you will not come, their minds may change.

CAESAR   How foolish do your fears seem now, Calphurnia! I will go.

A great crowd awaits outside the Capitol. There are shouts of 'Caesar! Caesar!' The shouts increase in volume and excitement. The faces of the crowd are joyful, eager. Caesar sees the soothsayer and approaches him, followed by Brutus, Cassius and the other conspirators.

CAESAR   The ides of March are come.

SOOTHSAYER   Ay, Caesar, but not gone.

Caesar shrugs his shoulders, and mounts the steps into the Capitol. The conspirators follow. A senator murmurs to Cassius.

SENATOR   I wish your enterprise today may thrive.

As he slips away, there is a great amount of nervous plucking at each other's sleeves and cloaks. The conspirators mutter to one another fearfully.

CASSIUS   I fear our purpose is discovered! Brutus, what shall be done?

BRUTUS   Cassius, be constant. Popilius Lena speaks not of our purposes, for look, he smiles, and Caesar doth not change.

CINNA   Casca, you are the first that rears your hand.

The conspirators encircle Caesar. Metellus kneels, then the others. Casca moves behind. As they kneel, they plead.

METELLUS   Most high, most mighty . . .

CINNA   O Caesar!

CASSIUS   Pardon, Caesar! Caesar, pardon!

Caesar, turning from one supplicant to another, pulls his clutched gown free.

BRUTUS   I kiss thy hand, but not in flattery, Caesar.

CAESAR   What Brutus?

DECIUS   Great Caesar!

CAESAR   Hence! Wilt thou lift up Olympus?

CASCA   Speak hands for me!

He stabs Caesar in the neck. The others rush upon the staggering Caesar and slash and stab at him. He continues to resist until he sees Brutus.

CAESAR   Et tu, Brute? – (*Seeing Brutus, Caesar covers his face with a gown in pitiful surrender.*) Then fall, Caesar!

Brutus strikes. Caesar dies, and falls at the base of Pompey's statue which has been splattered with blood. There is so much blood from Caesar and the wounded conspirators that it appears to spout blood, as in Calphurnia's dream. There is a moment of terrible silence.

CINNA   Liberty! Freedom! Tyranny is dead!

CASSIUS   Liberty! Freedom!

There is sudden turmoil in the senate, as the senators fly for their lives.

BRUTUS   Fly not, stand still, ambition's debt is paid!

But no one listens, and, presently, the conspirators are alone with their crime.

BRUTUS   Then walk we forth even to the market-place. Let's all cry, 'Peace, Freedom and Liberty!'.

As the conspirators kneel and smear their hands with blood, a shadow falls across them.

CASSIUS   Where is Mark Antony? (*He appears.*)

BRUTUS   Welcome, Mark Antony.

ANTONY   O mighty Caesar! dost thou lie so low? I know not, gentlemen, what you intend, who else must be let blood; if I myself there is no hour so fit as Caesar's death hour.

BRUTUS   O Antony! Beg not your death of us –

CASSIUS   Your voice shall be as strong as any man's in the disposing of new dignities.

BRUTUS   Only be patient till we have appeased the multitude, and then we will deliver you the cause why I, that did love Caesar when I struck him, have thus proceeded.

ANTONY   I doubt not of your wisdom. (*He shakes the conspirators' hands.*) And am, moreover, suitor that I may produce his body to the market-place, and in the pulpit, as becomes a friend, speak in the order of his funeral.

BRUTUS   You shall, Mark Antony.

CASSIUS   (*aside*) You know not what you do. Know you how much the people may be moved by that which he will utter?

BRUTUS   I will myself into the pulpit first, and show the reason of our Caesar's death.

CASSIUS   I know not what may fall; I like it not.

The conspirators leave. There is the roar of a crowd while Brutus speaks.

BRUTUS   Romans, countrymen, and lovers, hear me for my cause.

ANTONY   (*to Caesar's body*) Are all thy conquests, glories, triumphs, spoils, shrunk to this little measure? O pardon me, thou bleeding piece of earth, that I am meek and gentle with these butchers. Woe to the hand that shed this costly blood! (*He pauses.*) Cry havoc, and let slip the dogs of war!

Outside, Brutus addresses the people.

BRUTUS   As Caesar loved me, I weep for him; as he was valiant, I honour him; but, as he was ambitious, I slew him! (*There are loud cheers.*) I have the same dagger for myself, when it shall please my country to need my death!

ALL   Live, Brutus! live, live!

1ST PLEBEIAN   Bring him with triumph home unto his house!

2ND PLEBEIAN   Give him a statue –

3RD PLEBEIAN   Let him be Caesar!

Mark Antony enters, bearing Caesar's body. He lays it down on the ground. Brutus leaves.

ANTONY   Friends, Romans, countrymen, lend me your ears! I come to bury Caesar, not to praise him. The evil that men do lives after them, the good is oft interred with their bones. So let it be with Caesar. (*During the above, the crowd begins to stir and murmur.*) He was my friend, faithful and just to me; but Brutus says he was ambitious, and Brutus is an honourable man. When that the poor have cried, Caesar hath wept; ambition should be made of sterner stuff; yet Brutus says he was ambitious, and Brutus is an honourable man. You all did see I thrice presented him a kingly crown, which he did thrice refuse. Was this ambition?

1ST PLEBEIAN   Methinks there is much reason in his sayings.

2ND PLEBEIAN   Caesar has had great wrong.

3RD PLEBEIAN   I fear there will a worse come in his place.

4TH PLEBEIAN   There's not a nobler man in Rome than Antony!

The crowd begins to surge. The cry of 'Antony! Antony! Antony!' goes up.

ANTONY	If you have tears, prepare to shed them now. Look, in this place ran Cassius' dagger through; see what a rent the envious Casca made.
1ST PLEBEIAN	O piteous spectacle!
2ND PLEBEIAN	O noble Caesar!
ANTONY	Through this the well-beloved Brutus stabbed. This was the most unkindest cut of all.
4TH PLEBEIAN	O traitors, villains!
2ND PLEBEIAN	We will be revenged!
ALL	Revenge! Seek! Burn! Fire! Kill! Let not a traitor live!

The crowd, like a river in full spate, now bursts its banks and rushes through the streets, tearing up benches, and anything that comes in its way, shouting—

ALL	Away, away! Revenge, revenge!

They seize on a poor, unfortunate man. He struggles to be free.

CINNA THE POET	I am Cinna the poet! I am Cinna the poet! I am not Cinna the conspirator!

Cinna is dragged away, screaming.

ANTONY   (*watching the riot with grim satisfaction*) Now let it work.
Mischief, thou art afoot, take thou what course thou wilt.

*The conspirators flee from the fury of the people. Anyone
against whom there is the smallest suspicion is ruthlessly put to
death by order of Mark Antony and young Octavius, Caesar's
nephew and heir to his name. Brutus and Cassius escape into
Asia where they raise armies to march against Antony and
Octavius. But all is not well between the friends: Brutus
accuses Cassius of taking bribes.*

*Outside Brutus' tent, officers are listening, frowning and
worried. Within the tent, Brutus and Cassius confront one
another. Both are dressed for battle. Cassius looks the more
seasoned and professional.*

CASSIUS   I – an itching palm! When Caesar lived, he durst not thus have moved me.

BRUTUS   You durst not so have tempted him. (*With clenched fists*) Remember March, the ides of March remember. Did not great Julius bleed for justice' sake?

CASSIUS   Do not presume too much upon my love, I may do that I shall be sorry for.

BRUTUS   You have done that you should be sorry for.

CASSIUS   You love me not.

BRUTUS   I do not like your faults.

CASSIUS   A friendly eye could never see such faults.

BRUTUS   O Cassius, I am sick of many griefs. Portia is dead.

CASSIUS   How 'scaped I killing when I crossed you so? Upon what sickness?

BRUTUS   Impatient of my absence, and grief that young Octavius with Mark Antony have made themselves so strong; with this she fell distract and swallowed fire.

CASSIUS   Portia, art thou gone?

BRUTUS   No more, I pray you. I have here received letters that young
           Octavius and Mark Antony come down upon us with a mighty
           power. What think you of marching to Philippi presently?

CASSIUS   I do not think it good.

BRUTUS   Our cause is ripe. The enemy increaseth every day; we, at the
           height, are ready to decline. There is a tide in the affairs of
           men, which taken at the flood, leads on to fortune. And we
           must take the current when it serves.

CASSIUS   Then with your will, go on; we'll along ourselves, and meet
           them at Philippi.

           *Cassius leaves Brutus. The page, Lucius, is fast asleep in a
           corner. Brutus gently covers him and seats himself at his table.
           The yellow flame flickers, then begins to burn blue.*

           The ghost of Caesar enters.

BRUTUS   Ha! Who comes here? Art thou any thing? Speak to me what thou art!

GHOST   Thy evil spirit, Brutus.

BRUTUS   Why com'st thou?

GHOST   To tell thee thou shalt see me at Philippi.

BRUTUS   Well: then I shall see thee again?

GHOST   Ay.

The ghost vanishes.

On the plain of Philippi, Octavius and Mark Antony await the coming battle. Their great army stretches behind them. In the distance there is a faint glimmer of the enemy's steel.

SHAKESPEARE   THE ANIMATED TALES

ANTONY   Octavius, lead your battle softly on upon the left hand of the
            even field.

OCTAVIUS   Upon the right hand, I. Keep thou the left.

ANTONY   Why do you cross me?

OCTAVIUS   I do not cross you, but I will do so.

            Octavius and Antony return to their lines.
            Cassius confers with an officer.

CASSIUS   (*very sadly to an officer*) This is my birthday; as this very day
            was Cassius born. Be thou witness that against my will am I
            compelled to set upon one battle all our liberties. (*Brutus joins
            him.*) Now, most noble Brutus, if we lose this battle, are you
            contented to be led in triumph through the streets of Rome?

BRUTUS   No, Cassius, no. But this same day must end that work the ides
            of March begun. And whether we shall meet again I know not;
            for ever, and for ever, farewell, Cassius! If we do meet again,
            why, we shall smile; if not, why then this parting was well
            made.

CASSIUS   For ever, and for ever, farewell, Brutus! If we do meet again, we'll smile indeed; if not, 'tis true this parting was well made.

They ride away, together at first, then parting, one to the left, the other right.

The legions march towards one another. Then comes the clash of their meeting. There is violent fighting. The world is full of blood and dust, and the sounds of screams and howls, and blazing trumpets. All day long the battle raged. At last, the sun went down at Philippi. Antony and Octavius were victorious.

PINDARUS   Fly further off my lord. Mark Antony is in your tents.

CASSIUS   This day I breathed first; this is come round, and where I did begin, there shall I end. Caesar, thou art reveng'd, even with the sword that kill'd thee.

The battlefield darkens. Brutus bends over the dead body of Cassius who has killed himself rather than be captured.

The ghost of Caesar appears briefly and then fades away.

BRUTUS   O Julius Caesar, thou art mighty yet. (*He stares down.*) The last of all the Romans, fare thee well! Friends, I owe more tears to this dead man than you shall see me pay. I shall find time, Cassius, I shall find time. (*They all sit down.*) Our enemies have beat us to the pit. It is more worthy to leap in ourselves than tarry till they push us.

There are shouts in the distance and the approach of glimmering torches. Brutus bids farewell to his friends, all of whom leave save one, an old soldier by name of Strato.

BRUTUS   I know my hour is come. (*He runs on his sword.*) Caesar, now be still, I killed not thee with half so good a will.

He dies. The torches draw near.

The victorious Romans, Antony and Octavius, come upon the dead body of Brutus with Strato guarding it.

ANTONY   How died thy master, Strato?

STRATO   Brutus only overcame himself, and no man else hath honour by his death.

ANTONY   (*to Brutus*) This was the noblest Roman of them all: all the conspirators, save only he, did that they did in envy of great Caesar. He only, in a general honest thought and common good to all, made one of them. His life was gentle, and the elements so mixed in him that Nature might stand up and say to all the world, 'This was a man'.

The curtain falls.